Preface

This book will take you through the "Black" as well as the "White" part of the financial system .

Today many people as well as the institutions are so good at finance & financial systems , it is very easy for them to find loopholes and manipulate others .

This book will guide you how the manipulations in financial system works by white collar individuals and institutions

Foreword

" Finance means money and money means finance " This is the most simplified definition I can ever give to you.

Finance in general has no limitations when it comes to its sources and means. Almost every Person earns money from an ethical approach , few people don't.

This includes institutions as well as individuals. Since in today's time period people are having great knowledge of finance , they are also aware of the loopholes in the financial system .

About the author

This book has been written by Dhruv Jasbir Bansal , an NISM certified Research analyst (R.A) , AIWMI certified Alternative investments manager(AIM) & CWM candidate.

Dhruv bansal is an author of more than 8 books based on financial markets .

Dhruv bansal also teaches financial markets courses through his registered educational institute named sobarine finance institute .

Table of contents

- What is finance & financial system

- Basics of finance

- Sources of manipulation

- Financial crisis & Role of regulators

- Art of reading financial statements

- Financial intelligence

- Case studies of past events

- Conclusion

What is Finance & Financial system

"Finance in simple terms refers to money , its value , sources & means" .

Finance is required to fund a business , run a business & needed for survival of business . It is not only limited to business itself , every person on earth has a utility of finance & financial system .

From applying for a loan to startup funding , everyone is indeed dependent on finance .

Further we will look at what the financial system means and who all are the players in the financial system.

Financial system refers to the system where all the players in the segment contribute their part and form an ecosystem .

Financial system consists of the following ,

- Banks
- NBFC
- Investment banks & AMC
- Retail & institutional customers
- Accounting firms
- Regulatory bodies
- Financial markets intermediaries
- Central bank
- Finance ministry

Each player has its own role to play in the system and the system is incomplete without participation of each of the above players .

In today's time period , there are several ways to escape tax liabilities , regulations and law which has made it very difficult to operate with fair means .

Top tier institutions , major institutions and banks do their work whether with fair or unfair means but the scapegoat has always been a common investor / customer .

There were several events that led to a complete collapse of the entire financial system which left a mark on the system .

Now from misleading advertisements by investment firms to imposing unrealistic clauses in loan agreement & finding ways to deny claims on insurance policies every institution is focused on just one thing and that is to earn whether ethically or unethically .

Basics of finance

Finance is similar to an ocean , it goes deeper and deeper every time to try to understand and cannot be understood in one go .

But there are some basic concepts that can make you aware about its system and safeguard you from getting manipulated.

Following are few of its concepts that are very common in nature and you might get frequent encounters with it ,

1. Credit system of financial institutions
2. Mutual fund schemes
3. Fintech apps
4. Bank FD & CASA accounts

Credit system of financial institutions :

There are several credit systems in terms of institutional financing such as , leveraged buyouts , seed capital etc . but when it comes to retail customers following two are very common ,

- Loans
- Credit cards

Loans : There are various types of the retail loans , some of them are as follows ,

1. Personal loan
2. Educational loan
3. Vehicle loan
4. Housing loan
5. Marriage loan

In general terms , a loan is the credit facility that a bank usually offers in exchange of interest payments on loan amount .

There are several clauses in the loan agreement , be it of any kind/type . Since every person who takes the loan does not have adequate knowledge of finance and clauses of loan agreement it is also difficult for them to get through such situations .

Following are few clauses which should be understood by the retail consumer ,

Acceleration clause :

Meaning :

An accelerated clause is a term in a loan agreement that requires the borrower to pay off the loan immediately under certain conditions.

An accelerated clause is typically invoked when the borrower materially breaches the loan agreement.

Prepayment Fees and Penalties:

Meaning :

A prepayment penalty is a fee that some lenders charge if you pay off all or part of your mortgage early. If you have a prepayment penalty, you would have agreed to this when you closed on your home. Not all mortgages have a prepayment penalty

Predatory and usury :

Meaning :

Predatory lending practices, broadly defined, are the fraudulent, deceptive, and unfair tactics some people use to dupe us into mortgage loans that we can't afford.

Burdened with high mortgage debts, the victims of predatory lending can't spare the money to keep their houses in good repair.

Conclusion : The financial institutions will impose such clauses , whether with disclosures or without disclosures to the customers , so one should be vigilant and aware about such terms & conditions .

Credit cards :

It is the most widely used form of credit in the world. Almost every person has used a credit card in his lifetime.

Credit cards are issued by banks , NBFC , & credit card companies to the retail customers in which there is a certain credit cycle involved .

How do Credit Cards work online?

When you are paying for purchases online, the e-commerce store will ask you for the following details:

- Choose whether it is Visa or Mastercard
- 16-digit card number,
- Expiry date,
- CVV
- Name as printed on the card
- Billing address (sometimes)

Once you hit pay, the information is sent to your bank via a payment gateway.

The bank sends an OTP or one-time password to your registered email ID or mobile number to authenticate the transaction. If the OTP is correct, then your transaction is complete.

So we now know the answers to two questions: how do Credit Cards work, and how Credit Card payments work. Now let's look at some of the terminologies that will help you understand how credit cards work.

Interest: This is an essential aspect of how Credit Cards work. By using a Credit Card, you are taking money on credit from the issuer. It's a bit like a loan, on which you may have to pay interest.

However, this is applicable only if you don't pay the entire bill that you get. If you leave some amount pending, you will be charged interest on it.

Another thing you need to understand about how Credit Cards work is that the interest charged is every month, and not on an annual one.

For example, the interest charged could be 3 percent a month, or around 36 percent a year.

Credit limit: Every Credit Card has an upper limit beyond which you cannot spend. If you try to use the card after you've reached the upper limit, the transaction may be rejected by the Credit Card issuer.

Various factors determine the credit limit – the type of Credit Card that you have, your income and ability to pay, any other debts that you may have, your credit score and your record of prompt payments.

If your record is good, the Credit Card issuer will give you the option of increasing the Credit Card limit.

Billing cycle: This is the fixed period in which you can make purchases until you get the bill.

If you make purchases at the beginning of the cycle, you will have a longer time of credit – that is you get more time before you pay for the transactions.

Minimum payment: There is a minimum amount that you have to pay on your Credit Card bill.

If you don't do that, you could pay a charge for it. You can carry forward any amount that is more than the minimum amount, but you will have to pay interest on it.

Balance: Balance is the sum you've spent using your Credit Card, but haven't paid back yet.

Payment decoupling :

'Credit card' is the perfect example to understand this ,
when you use cash you already know how much cash you
have already ,So you use the cash very wisely.

In the case of a credit card you are lenient , you would be
using according to your need or habit

So payment decoupling is the instance of higher spending
on credit cards than a person would spend by using cash.

Maximum 40 % interest is charged when you default on the payment of credit cards . Nominal interest rate is 3-15% which varies from company to company .

It is very easy to perform a transaction , but very difficult to repay if you do not have financial stability so it's better to use debit cards instead of credit cards which will ensure you will not get into "Debt trap".

Mutual fund schemes :

Mutual fund schemes are collective investment vehicles , These are managed by specialized professionals called fund managers .

Unlike equity investments , the mutual fund scheme does not offer ownership & voting rights to the investor .

These schemes are a low cost investment option for the common retail investor and the basic capital requirements start with as low as RS 500 .

There are two methods to invest , one time investment & SIP . In case of one time , you are paying a lump sum amount to acquire certain units of the scheme in one transaction only.

In case of SIP you are investing in the schemes on a regular basis , monthly , weekly or quarterly .

A certain amount which an investor intends to invest is automatically deducted from their account and gets invested in the schemes in which they have started the schemes .

Example : An sip of Rs 500 monthly , in tax saver ELSS fund. Here RS 500 will be deducted from the savings account of the investor and will be used to buy certain units of the fund.

Issues with mutual fund investments which an investor must know ,

1. Misleading advertisements
2. Returns over investment
3. Fund manager tactics
4. Lock-in
5. Fund structure and "risk-o-meter"

Misleading advertisements :

Few mutual fund companies showcase their schemes in a falsifying manner to attract investors to invest in their schemes.

This includes giving unrealistic returns promises and showcases of past returns which is not a guarantee for future returns at all. The investor must be aware of such misleading ads .

Returns of investment :

Most of the mutual schemes advertisements include the term "past returns / performance" over 1 year in their email marketing and social media marketing .

This concept of past returns is highly unrealistic in nature, because the past is not a promise of future in financial markets specifically.

These fictitious ads must be tackled with the use of CAGR instead of one year performance . it removes biases and gives the actual compounding return information .

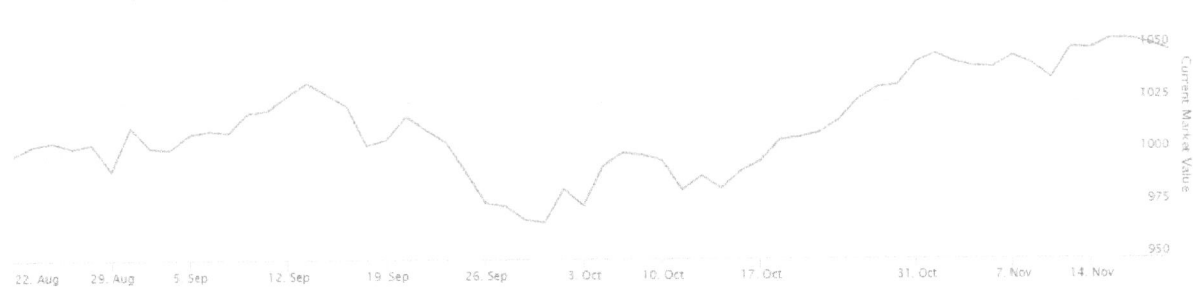

The Value of Lumpsum ∨ of ₹ 1000 ∨ invested 3 Months back ∨ would now be ₹1049.11

As you can see these companies advertise it in " your X amount would have been today Y amount " manner.

Now let me explain this graph in a simple way which a new investor could relate to .

22. Aug   29. Aug   5. Sep   12. Sep   19. Sep   26. Sep

From 22 aug to 26 sep NAV fell from 1000 to 967. Now when an investor does not have any knowledge about the markets , he will get panicked and sell after seeing a loss of 33 per unit .

This concept of variable returns is smoothly hidden by mutual fund companies and specially so called "Agents". If an uneducated person invests thinking he will get good returns and later see such loss it is difficult to stay invested for him .

Fund manner tactics :

Fund managers are paid incentives , performance fees , AUM fees apart from their salaries . Few fund managers in the desperation of money , "churn portfolios" .

This refers to frequent transactions with an intention to earn incentives , whether the scheme has or has not given any returns to the investors .

In 2022 there was a recent event of Axis mutual fund , front running scam.

It was alleged that the two fund managers allegedly made illicit gains through front-running. However, the Axis AMC did not elaborate on the violations that led to the two fund managers' sacking.

Lock-in period :

This refers to the imposition of a clause which forces investors to compulsorily stay invested in the scheme. Investors must check if there is any lock-in or not .

The lock-in is usually of 3 years , and the investor cannot sell his units in these three years . Which means these scheme lacks liquidity .

Fund structure and "risk-o-meter" :

Fund structure is generally the composition of the scheme portfolio of securities . And the risk-o-meter shows the risk involved in the scheme of mutual funds .

A fund can be structured in any manner depending on the type of scheme , like equity , debt , hybrid etc .

For example in a hybrid scheme , there could be 30% debt and 70% equity or in any other composition as mentioned in scheme disclosures .

Risk-o-meter shows the level of risk involved ,

RISKOMETER

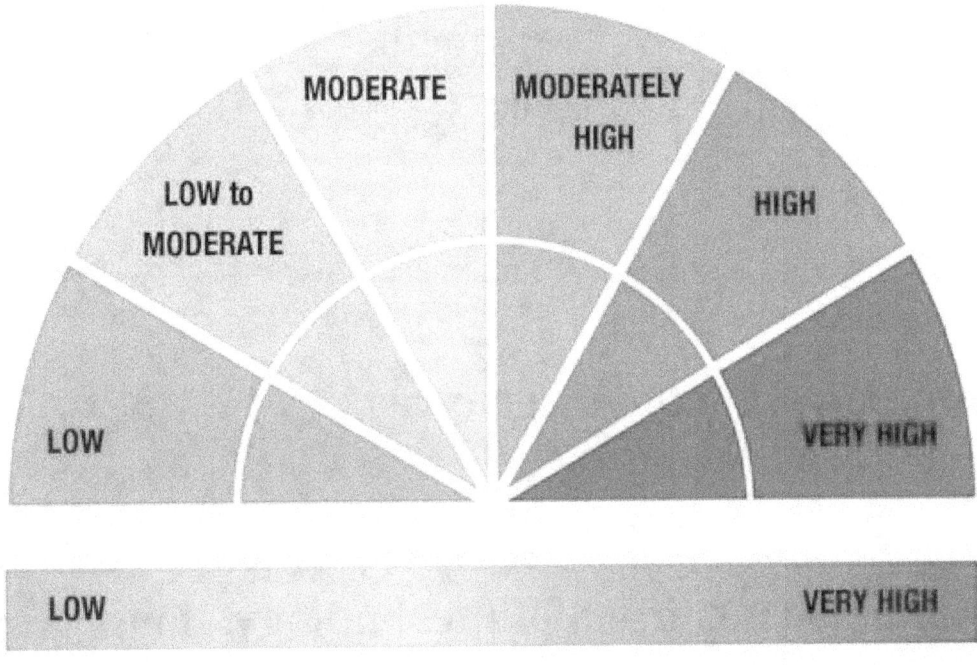

One should always check the level of risk involved .

Fintech apps

Post 2017 the fintech industry had seen a very significant growth in consumer base as well as revenues. There are several types of fintech companies ,

1. Payment infrastructure / gateways
2. Credit / loans
3. Stock broking & investments
4. Trading / forex / crypto

Payment infrastructures / gateways :

This refers to the UPI payment apps , these apps offer cashless payments from UPI technology along with other features .

Few players like paytm are involved in lending business which is generally unsecured and short term in nature .

In 2022 RBI stopped onboarding of paytm payment bank new customers and investigated against breach of policies and regulations .

Fintech apps are not as regulated as banks & financial institutions and are often seen exploiting customers' data privacy .

Fintech apps charge high commissions on mobile recharge , flight tickets etc . These services when availed directly from the company are free of any commissions .

Credit / loans :

Many fintech apps offer credit / loan facilities . These apps claim to give up to 3 lakhs in unsecured form.

Many cases were filed against several fintech apps which called customers and abused them to repay and threatened them .

Many Chinese fintech apps were banned in India due to frauds , harassment and money laundering .
Even paytm was accused of selling customer data to its chinese investor firms .

So it's better to stay away from such debt traps . Getting credit / loans is very easy but to repay with such interest rates and clauses is very difficult .

Stock broking & investments :

There are several players in the stock broking and investments industry including small fintechs to large corporations .

There are several fintech apps which lure clients and trap them into investing their money into the schemes they are promoting .

Against many fintech apps SEBI has initiated investigations and canceled their broking license.
Few of the fintech apps such as phonepe , paytm offer their users to invest in sip which they promote .

Here the investor is not aware about the financial markets and then too many invest without due diligence, which leads to either losses or minimizing their gains.

Bank FD & CASA accounts :

Bank FD is a very secured form of investing money , but with a very minimal return . Most of the people who are unaware about the other investment options prefer to invest in FD .

The average interest rate is around 4 to 6 % yearly. If the only motive of a customer is to safeguard his money then it is one of the best options .

But if the motive of the consumer is to earn a return then it's not an ideal option , since the returns are very minimal.

Banks present it in such a manner that customers become keen to invest in such an option , but do not tell you about the actual inflation adjusted return you are entitled to and post deduction of TDS .

CASA (current account savings account) : many people who are salaried class let their money stay into their savings account on which interest rate is 2-3% yearly .

In the case of a current account no interest is paid on balance .

So one should be vigilant while planning to invest their money in any available option .

Sources of manipulations

There are several ways a company could manipulate others , the most prominent method for them is through financial statements .

Financial statements depict the state of financial stability for a given company , when companies cannot perform well , they try to cover up such things through adjusting financial statements in a manner which seems realistic .

There are several ways a company can mislead you with their financial statements which we will see further .

Misusing the Flexibility Given for Creating Provisions & Reserves :

The most common way of fudging financial statements is by creating provisions and reserves. Here the companies take advantage of the flexibility given by the accounting standards.

The standards allow management to estimate and make assumptions for future bad debts, receivables, and other accrued income. But instead, some manipulators use this to their advantage to distort earnings.

Personally, we feel that this practice is very common in the case of Banking, Housing loans, and financial companies in India.

In the case of banks, the senior management has full flexibility to make assumptions about non-performing assets (NPA).

Higher provisioning done in one quarter can lead to lower profits in that quarter and vice versa.

Therefore whenever the bank wants to improve its earnings it can delay the recognition of bad debts.

This is done by creating fewer provisions in that financial year/quarter and thereby tweaking its earnings.

Overstating Earnings :

The other common method of manipulating statements is through overstating earnings by showing fictitious sales and advance revenues.

This strategy is very common in manufacturing companies.

Companies do this by showing inflated sales, advanced sales without an actual sale of goods, or recognizing revenue in one go instead of actually breaking it up for the duration of the project or period of sale.

This practice is commonly used by real estate companies to manipulate sales

Related Party Transactions :

Companies indulge in related party transactions to divert company funds. These diverted funds are sent to offshore accounts through dummy companies. These accounts are operated by relatives or close family members of the promoter.

An e.g. of this is a company granting loans to relatives of promoters.

The company then claims them as bad debts thereby removing company funds belonging to shareholders.

Another common tactic used is selling items at higher prices to related parties to inflate sales. These parties are then given a share of the differential amount.

Therefore as an investor one should take a good look at the related party transactions of the company as disclosed in the annual report.

Underreporting Costs and Expenses or Delaying it :

Companies also shift current expenses to a later period. This delays expense recognition and therefore pushes the earnings on an upward trajectory.

Companies capitalizing normal operational costs which should directly appear in the P/L statement.

This is done to reduce costs. These costs are then shifted to the balance sheet.This is also a usual way for companies to alter their financial statements.

Creative Accounting Practices:

Some of the procedures and practices shown as examples of creative accounting practices can be listed as follows:

a) Creating fictitious income or booking income without accrual.

b) Aggressive capitalization of interest expenses or extension of the depreciation period.

c) False disclosure of assets and liabilities.

d)   Changing the classification of income statement items through transactions such as showing extraordinary income as operating income and operating expenses as extraordinary expenses.

e)   To present the cash generated business from investments or other activities in the cash flow statement as cash generated from operations in order to create the impression that the company has a high cash generating power.

Off balance sheet manipulations :

Common forms of off-balance-sheet financing include operating leases and partnerships. Operating leases have been widely used, although accounting rules have been tightened to lessen the use.

 A company can rent or lease a piece of equipment and then buy the equipment at the end of the lease period for a minimal amount of money, or it can buy the equipment outright.

Off balance sheet Special Purpose Vehicles (SPVs), allow a company to move assets and liabilities off a company's balance sheet, whilst still potentially using those assets.

If you can transfer an asset off your balance sheet to a separate entity for more that the value it's sitting on your books, then you can potentially recognise that difference as a gain in earnings.

Andrew Fastow, once the CFO to Enron, is the off-balance sheet vehicle legend. At Enron he created 3,000 separate, off balance sheet, corporate entities.

Fastow used the SPVs for a variety of purposes, including collateralizing debt and moving impaired assets. In simple terms, he created a web so complex that it was impossible to discern the true liability position of Enron and enabled him to inflate earnings.

According to International Financial Reporting Standards if a company (parent) controls an entity (a subsidiary), then consolidated financial statements need preparing.

That is to say, all the assets and liabilities of the parent and subsidiary SPVs are added together into one set of accounts.

So if a company retains control of an SPV then the consolidation defeats the purpose of the arrangement, ie. the asset and liability would still show on the consolidated balance sheet.

A common use of the SPV's was for Enron to sell assets at above their book values (the values in the balance sheet) to the SPVs. Selling an asset at above book value can results in a gain, which potentially goes to the income statement, ie. increasing earnings.

In 2001 Enron filed for bankruptcy, which was then the largest in history (until WorldCom's bankruptcy a year later).

Fastow pleaded guilty to two charges of conspiracy and was sentenced to ten years with no parole.

While Enron was imploding, an email was sent round to Andersen staff about document retention policy, which led to the shredding of thousands of documents.

This resulted in Andersens being charged with obstruction of justice (the conviction was subsequently overturned). This, amongst other failings, led to the downfall of Andersens and its 80,000 employees.

Crypto currencies :

These are also referred to as digital currencies and there is extremely high speculative activities involved with these digital assets .

The crypto does not have any underlying asset and is highly speculative in nature with absolutely zero intrinsic value .

Most of the teenagers are involved in such trading activities either influenced by so called youtubers or by their non informative friends .

Crypto currency is a sheer waste of time and resources and this has been said by legendary investors like Warren Buffett , Charlie Munger and many other veteran investors.

Since there is no actual underlying asset the real value of these assets are 0 and there could not be any cash flow generation as well .

There have been many incidents with the apps that allow you to trade in crypto since they are not regulated by the financial markets watchdog or even the central banking regulations .

Many actions were taken in the past with various crypto apps , in relation to fraudulent activities carried with investors money .

Many apps denied to return deposits of money contributed by investors and in some cases they duped investors with fake virtual trading accounts .

Few apps in the past have cheated investors by saying the server was hacked and they are not giving the deposits back to investors .

It's better to invest in highly regulated and liquid assets such as equity & bonds .

Financial crisis & role of regulators

Financial crisis:

There were various events of the financial crisis in the past whether global or country specific crisis . Each had given a lesson to learn from .

From the great depression of 1932 to current year 2022, The financial & economic participants haven't learnt anything from previous events .

Every participant knows the economic outcome of certain decisions they make , still without thinking about the future, they repeat such acts willingly .

Today everything works on "Debt" and this has become a harsh reality .

Business enterprises raise funding through debt capital ,
government finances projects on debt & people use credit
cards for shopping .

To some extent debt capital is a very realistic and
beneficial form of raising capital , but with the growth of
startup culture , now every enterprise looks forward to
funding their business with too much debt .

Now there are frequent economic turmoils due to a simple
fact: business entities raising debt > defaulting on
obligations > causing banking failures > forcing banks to
take credit from central banks > increase in inflation >
end result : economic slowdowns / turmoil .

Business debt funding is not the only reason , there are
various other reasons like failure of central banks in
controlling economic conditions & excess credit creation.

Role of regulators :

Each nation has its own regulators for banking systems , financial markets etc.

Now with a failure of one , will lead to a domino effect and will affect other systems .

Banking regulators ie. central banks are the most crucial institution responsible for credit & economic control in a nation .

When the central bank is burdened by the political parties, it may be forced to make decisions which create economic disruption for a nation and this is the same for every nation.

Art of reading financial statements

Financial statements are a ' mirror' of quantitative performance of any firm , Further we would be looking at the elaboration of these statements and their components.

- Quarterly Results

- Profit & Loss

- Balance Sheet

- Cash Flows

- Shareholding Pattern

Quarterly Results :

 A quarterly report is a summary or collection of unaudited financial statements, such as balance sheets, income statements, and cash flow statements, issued by companies every quarter (three months). Quarterly reports are typically filed within a few weeks of a quarter's end.

Quarterly Results

Consolidated Figures in Rs. Crores / View Standalone

	Sep 2018	Dec 2018	Mar 2019	Jun 2019	Sep 2019	Dec 2019	Mar 2020	Jun 2020
Sales +	54	46	51	58	53	54	60	65
Expenses +	21	24	23	36	28	38	34	27
Operating Profit	33	22	28	23	25	16	26	38
OPM %	61%	49%	55%	39%	47%	30%	43%	58%
Other Income	10	16	18	15	17	14	13	21
Interest	0	0	0	0	0	0	0	0
Depreciation	2	3	3	3	3	3	3	2
Profit before tax	40	36	43	35	38	27	36	56
Tax %	25%	22%	21%	20%	24%	21%	21%	17%
Net Profit	30	28	34	27	29	21	29	46
EPS in Rs	2.87	2.69	3.21	2.62	2.80	1.99	2.74	4.42

Above is the quarterly result of CDSL LTD

Following are the components of the quarterly results,

- Sales
- Expenses
- Operating profit
- Opm
- Other income
- Interest
- Depreciation
- Profit before tax
- Tax
- Net profit

Further , We would be looking at the meaning and definitions of these components of the quarterly result.

Sales :

Is a term used to describe the activities that lead to the selling of goods or services. Businesses have sales organizations that are broken up into different teams. And these sales teams are often determined based on the region they're selling to, the product or service they're selling, and the target customer.

Quarterly Sales plays an important role in identifying the financial strength of a company. There are certain things that need to be clear when you read the sales figure of any firm.

Following are the ideal points to look in the sales of the company ,

- sales of recent quarter should be greater than previous quarter
- Growth should be seen in the sales figure of the most recent 5 quarters
- Sales should not be decreased in the recent quarters

Expenses : Following expenses can be seen in a company ,

- Salesperson salaries and wages.
- Sales administrative staff salaries and wages.
- Commissions.
- Payroll taxes.
- Benefits.
- Travel and entertainment.
- Facility rent / showroom rent.
- Depreciation

The type of expenses may vary , depending on the type of company . We need to focus on the legitimacy of the expense ie. if they were really valid for the firm.

Expenses should be decreased over the time or have to stay neutral , it should not be increased over the time for any firm.

Operating profit :

Operating Profit = Gross Profit – Operating Expenses – Depreciation – Amortization.

A company's operating profit is its total earnings from its core business functions for a given period, excluding the deduction of interest and taxes.

It also excludes any profits earned from ancillary investments, such as earnings from other businesses that a company has a part interest in.

Along with quarterly sales , operating profit should also increase every quarter , and should show adequate growth.

Operating profit margin :

Operating Profit Margin is a profitability or performance ratio that reflects the percentage of profit a company produces from its operations, prior to subtracting taxes and interest charges.

It is an essential profitability ratio which is seen in the % format.

It shows how much profitability efficiency a firm is having after deducting the expenses out of it.

Example : CESC LTD has quoted 24 % as it's OPM as on June 2021 quarter.

Usually finance and IT firms have high OPM and steel and power sector firms have low OPM.

Other income : Other income is income that does not come from a company's main business, such as interest.

Examples of other income include income from interest, rent, and gains resulting from the sale of fixed assets.

Following are the sources of other income ,

- REVENUE FORM SUBSIDIARIES
- REVENUE FROM SALE OF ASSET
- INTEREST / DIVIDEND

Any firm should try to increase the sales , not the revenue from other income.

Since the sales revenue is the income generated by the parent firm and other income is generated by subsidiary firms , it is essential for the other income to not exceed the sales revenue itself.

Interest : An interest expense is the cost incurred by an entity for borrowed funds. Interest expense is a non-operating expense shown on the income statement.

It represents interest payable on any borrowings – bonds, loans, convertible debt or lines of credit.

Every firm borrows funds or raise debt for meeting the capital requirements , therefore debt is a part and parcel of business

Since a company borrows or raises funds , they have to return it in the form of interest. Therefore a firm has to efficiently return the debt in the form of interest.

NOTE : Banks and financial institutions have normally high interest expenses due to high amounts of debt and borrowings.

Depreciation : In accountancy, depreciation refers to two aspects of the same concept: first, the actual decrease of fair value of an asset, such as the decrease in value of factory equipment each year as it is used .

Every firm has assets such as machinery , furniture and equipment , therefore it is rational that its value would decrease over its lifetime.

In the quarterly results you can have an insight into how much a company is facing depreciation on its assets .

It is essential that a firm should not face very high amounts of depreciation over its assets.

Depreciation example :

Following are the examples for depreciation ,

Example 1 : CYIENT LTD

The firm had depreciation of RS 49 CR as of June 2021 quarter .

Example 2 : BHARTI AIRTEL LTD

The firm had depreciation of RS 7741 CR as of June 2021 quarter .

Depreciation varies from company to company and sector to sector , a finance firm would have less depreciation and a steel company would have very high depreciation.

Profit before tax :

Profit before tax is a measure that looks at a company's profits before the company has to pay corporate income tax.

It essentially is all of a company's profits without the consideration of any taxes.

Profit before tax can be found on the income statement as operating profit minus interest.

Profit before tax is an essential factor that needs to be understood while analyzing quarterly statements , it shows the amount earned before any applicable tax on the firm.

Since tax is also an essential part to be considered , you need to know the financial strength of the firm prior to it too.

TAX :

A tax is a mandatory fee or financial charge levied by any government on an individual or an organization to collect revenue for public works providing the best facilities and infrastructure.

The collected fund is then used to fund different public expenditure programs.

Tax applicable would differ from company to company, since every firm has different operations and business functions as well as sectors , tax rate might differ.

Example 1 : QUICK HEAL TECHNOLOGIES LTD,

The firm had paid tax of 15.92 % on it's revenue as on June 2021 quarter.

Example 2 : HFCL LTD ,The firm has paid 27 % tax on it's revenue as of June 2021 quarter .

Net profit :

Synonymous with net income, net profit is a company's total earnings after subtracting all expenses.

Expenses subtracted include the costs of normal business operation as well as depreciation and taxes.

Net profit is commonly referred to as a company's "bottom line" and is a true indicator of a company's profitability.

You can consider that this is the final amount , company earns after the end of a certain period .

Example 1:

FEDERAL BANK LTD

The bank quoted net profit of RS 357 CR as of June 2021 quarter .

Example 2 :

SRF LTD

The firm quoted net profit of RS 395 CR as of June 2021 quarter .

Profit & loss statement :

An income statement or profit and loss account is one of the financial statements of a company and shows the company's revenues and expenses during a particular period. It indicates how the revenues are transformed into the net income or net profit.

Profit & Loss

Consolidated Figures in Rs. Crores / View Standalone

	Mar 2010	Mar 2011	Mar 2012	Mar 2013	Mar 2014	Mar 2015	Mar 2016	Mar 2017	Mar 2018	Ma
Sales +	4,625	5,140	5,490	6,873	18,802	22,621	26,494	29,141	30,773	
Expenses +	3,495	3,721	4,572	5,451	14,630	18,428	22,234	24,956	26,063	
Operating Profit	1,131	1,419	918	1,422	4,172	4,193	4,260	4,184	4,710	
OPM %	24%	28%	17%	21%	22%	19%	16%	14%	15%	
Other Income	69	-298	30	-141	244	106	453	775	1,417	
Interest	218	100	103	103	80	69	97	129	162	
Depreciation	134	144	161	200	522	611	759	978	1,085	
Profit before tax	847	877	685	978	3,815	3,618	3,857	3,853	4,879	
Tax %	17%	15%	21%	24%	20%	27%	22%	26%	22%	
Net Profit	700	644	1,096	1,288	3,029	2,628	2,993	2,813	3,800	
EPS in Rs	14.32	12.79	21.48	25.13	32.44	27.35	30.92	28.88	38.78	
Dividend Payout %	6%	8%	5%	5%	15%	22%	35%	28%	33%	

The only difference between quarterly results and P&l statement is the duration of the statement , P&L statement is issued over 1 YR period and quarterly results are issued every 3 months

Balance sheet : In financial accounting, a balance sheet is a summary of the financial balances of an individual or organization, whether it be a sole proprietorship, a business partnership, a corporation, private limited company or other organization such as a government or not-for-profit entity.

Balance Sheet

Consolidated Figures in Rs. Crores / View Standalone

	Mar 2012	Mar 2013	Dec 2013	Mar 2015	Mar 2016	Mar 2017
Share Capital +	30	30	96	26	113	127
Reserves	23	38	88	226	243	1,178
Borrowings	56	88	64	224	393	779
Other Liabilities +	163	193	227	244	500	780
Total Liabilities	254	331	398	719	1,250	2,864
Fixed Assets +	32	33	85	129	252	1,172
CWIP	-0	-0	-0	-0	2	8
Investments	-0	-0	-0	-0	4	78
Other Assets +	222	297	313	590	992	1,607
Total Assets	254	331	398	719	1,250	2,864

Above is the balance sheet of QUESS CORP LTD, There are several components in the balance sheet that we will see further .

Components of balance sheet : Following are the components of the balance sheet ,

- Share Capital
- Reserves
- Borrowings
- Other Liabilities
- Total Liabilities
- Fixed Assets
- CWIP
- Investments
- Other Assets
- Total Assets

We will further see the meaning and definition of these components of the balance sheet.

Share capital :

A firm's share capital or capital stock is the portion of a corporation's equity that has been obtained by the issue of shares in the corporation to a shareholder.

"Share capital" may also denote the number and types of shares that compose a corporation's share structure.

In simple terms share capital denotes sources of funds , structure of funds that are in the form of equity capital , or preference shares capital.

It is essential for the investor to analyze the capital structure of the firm and its efficiency.

ROE is the financial ratio that shows efficiency of a firm in delivering returns to the shareholders of the company .

Reserves :

Also known as retained earnings are portions of a business's profits which have been set aside to strengthen the business's financial position.

Reserves are often used to purchase fixed assets; to repay debts; or to fund expansions, bonus, and dividend repayments.

Reserves are important for the firm and it should be properly utilized by the firm without any foul-play.

There should be growth in reserves over the time for the firm. It is necessary for the firm to show growth in the reserves for future expansion and company growth.

Borrowings :

Borrowings are classified as current liabilities unless the Group has an unconditional right to postpone settlement of the liability for, or the liability is due to be settled at least 12 months after the balance sheet date.

In simple terms you can consider the borrowings as liability that is a company liable / obligated to pay back to the creditor.

Therefore the borrowings should be decreased by the firm over time . If the firm does not pay back the borrowings efficiently then , interest would lapse and get harmful for financial stability of the firm.

Current liabilities are required to returned to creditors within one year and long term debt can be returned after several years depending on the term of loan

Other liabilities :

Other current liabilities, in financial accounting, are categories of short-term debt that are lumped together on the liabilities side of the balance sheet. The term "current liabilities" refers to items of short-term debt that a firm must pay within 12 months.

In simple terms , other liability is the remaining liabilities that are not mentioned in the balance sheet liability section.

Definition :

"Other liabilities" on a balance sheet is a general category of debts or obligations that don't fit into the other categories listed.

This category is used to ensure the company is listing all of its debts and obligations for shareholders and other interested parties.

Total liabilities :

Definition " Total liabilities are the aggregate debt and financial obligations owed by a business to individuals and organizations at any specific period of time".

Total liabilities are reported on a company's balance sheet and are a component of the general accounting equation:

= Liabilities + Equity.

You can view this as an end point of the liabilities section in the balance sheet , This is the section where there is sum total of the all types of liabilities / borrowing and debt taken and raised by the firm.

Note :

Liabilities of the firm should decrease over the time period but whereas in case of banks it should increase as it shows deposit of funds by the clients.

Fixed assets :

Now we will move towards the assets section in the balance sheet .

Fixed assets are " long-term assets that a company has purchased and is using for the production of its goods and services ".

Fixed assets include property, plant, and equipment (PP&E) and are recorded on the balance sheet.

Fixed assets are also referred to as tangible assets, meaning they're physical assets.

Fixed assets play an important role in any firm as they are " tangible assets " .

High Fixed assets also have one drawback and that is depreciation that gets accumulated over the period of time.

Example :

BHARTI AIRTEL LTD has reported depreciation worth : RS 163,942 as on march 2021.

CWIP (Capital work in progress) :

The Capital Work in Progress, also known in short as CWIP, is one of the important parts of the non-current asset of an entity.

CWIP includes building under construction, machinery under assembly etc., at the time of preparation of balance sheet.

CWIP is the work that is not yet complete but the amount has already been paid.

It is important for any firm to have less amount of CWIP as this portion of the capital has been invested but the outcome hasn't arrived yet (returns on investment) .

In most of the cases infrastructure and development firms have high amounts of CWIP and finance institutions have low or no CWIP.

Investments : This portion of the balance sheet shows the investments done by the firm in order to generate short term / long term returns.

This basically shows how much a firm invests in highly liquid securities of other firms listed on the stock exchange or off the market securities that could be quickly converted into cash.

A firm with high investments also shows its liquidity nature , this attracts a high number of investors .

Example : EXIDE INDUSTRIES LTD , has a market capitalization of RS 15,678 CR and has investments worth RS 19,340 CR .

Other assets :

Definition " Other assets is a grouping of accounts that is listed as a separate line item in the assets section of the balance sheet ".

This line item contains minor assets that do not naturally fit into any of the main asset categories, such as current assets or fixed assets .

You can simply understand that assets which cannot be specifically categorized are included in other assets .

Example :

ASIAN PAINTS LTD ha other assets worth RS 9,577 CR

Total assets :

Definition " Total assets refers to the sum of the book values of all assets owned by an individual, company, or organization " .

It is a parameter that is often used in net worth debt covenants. The value of a company's total assets is obtained after accounting for depreciation. associated with the assets.

This section of the balance sheet shows an aggregate view of all the assets of a firm , current or non current both.

It is important to properly view and understand the various sections / parts of the balance sheet as it tells us what is the underlying financial situation in the firm.

Cash Flow statement :

In simple terms, a cash flow statement is nothing but a statement that shows movement of funds inside-out the firm.

Basically cash flow statement can be divided into three segments/parts , following are the three parts of cash flow statement ,

- Cash from operating activities

- Cash from investing activities

- Cash from financing activities

Cash Flow statements play a very important role in understanding various movements of cash in a firm. We will be looking at various types of cash flows .

Cash from operating activities :

Definition " Cash from operating activities usually refers to the first section of the statement of cash flows. "

Cash from operating activities focuses on the cash inflows and outflows from a company's main business activities of buying and selling merchandise, providing services, etc.

You can consider this type of cash flow as a statement showing inflow and outflow of funds derived from the workflow/operations of the business and could be an essential factor to be analyzed in any type of firm

	Mar 2010	Mar 2011	Mar 2012	Mar 2013	Mar 2014
Cash from Operating Activity -	108	64	100	120	103
Profit from operations	146	147	215	328	405
Receivables	49	-82	-144	-44	-205
Inventory	0	0	0	0	-3
Payables	-49	35	51	15	-18
Loans Advances	-17	-18	-6	-22	-8
Other WC items	0	7	11	-57	62
Working capital changes	-17	-57	-87	-108	-173
Direct taxes	-21	-25	-27	-100	-129
Other operating items	0	-0	-0	0	0

Above is the operating cash flow statement of Birlasoft Ltd from the year 2010 - 2017.

As you can see there is an inflow of cash that is shown in (+ve) and the expenditures and spending of the firm is shown in (-ve) sign .

This statement shows the basic operational activities of the firm along with movement of funds related to it.

Cash from investing activities :

Definition " Cash flow from investing activities is the cash that has been generated (or spent) on non-current assets that are intended to produce a profit in the future. "

Types of activities that this may include are capital expenditures, lending money, and sale of investment securities. Following are included in the statement ,

- Purchase of property, plant, and equipment (PP&E), also known as capital expenditures.
- Proceeds from the sale of PP&E.
- Acquisitions of other businesses or companies.
- Proceeds from the sale of other businesses (divestitures)
- Purchases of marketable securities (i.e., stocks, bonds, etc.)

Cash from financing activities :

Definition : " Cash flow from financing activities (CFF) is a section of a company's cash flow statement, which shows the net flows of cash that are used to fund the company. "

Financing activities include transactions involving debt, equity, and dividends.

Cash from Financing Activity -	-16	-2,746	-1,719	-1,140	-3,570
Proceeds from shares	8	0	0	1	1
Proceeds from borrowings	6,343	7,260	7,084	0	0
Repayment of borrowings	-5,566	-8,380	-6,990	0	0
Interest paid fin	-119	-70	-90	-85	-94
Dividends paid	-682	-1,558	-1,723	-1,707	-2,329
Financial liabilities	0	0	0	0	0
Share application money	0	0	0	0	0
Application money refund	0	-2	0	0	0
Other financing items	1	4	1	651	-1,148

Statement above is of Wipro Ltd from 2010 -2017

Shareholding pattern :

This statement contains details about the stakes of partners & promoters of the firm on yearly basis as well as on quarterly basis.

In order to sustain and maintain high efficiency of management it is important that the shareholding statement/pattern should be stable and do not show much movement in a shorter duration ,

And in that case there would be a sense of disbelief caused amongst the investors of the firm.

The shareholding statement shows about the stakes owned in firm by ,

- PROMOTERS
- FIIS
- DIIS
- PUBLIC

Promoters :

This shows the stakes owned by the founders ,
management and other associates in the firm.

Ideally the % of holding by the promoters should be from
40% to 75% , Promoter holding showcase the
trustworthiness of the management and it's efficiency .

If the promoter holding is less than 40% then it shows the
lack of participation in the ownership of the firm by the
founders and management .

In case the promoter holding is more than 75 , then it
shows lack of liquidity and free float shares for the public
/ retail investors.

Changes in promoter holding shows many indications for the investors.

If it has increased then it shows that the firm is supposed to perform well in the near future and participation of management is increased in the firm and vis-à-vis.

FIIS :

This part of the statement shows the stakes owned by the foreign institutional investors , amc , holding firms etc.

Increase in this part shows the interest in the firm shown by the " Smart money ".

DIIS :

This part usually shows the stakes owned by the financial institutions in which the company has been incorporated.

Increase and decrease of the stakes is an important factor for the firm .

Public :

This part of the statement shows the stakes owned by the HNI who have substantially invested an amount to take a % of stake in the firm along with the shares held by the retail investors .

Peer comparison / competitive analysis :

It is very essential for any investor whether an HNI or retail investor to do the peer comparison/competitive analysis .

This method comprises of 2 basic steps ,

- Identifying the industry / sector of firm
- Analyzing firms in that industry / sector.

1) Identifying the industry / sector of the firm : It is a very simple step which tells you about the firm's industry/sector.

Example: INFOSYS LTD ,

SECTOR : IT

INDUSTRY : SOFTWARE

COMPETITORS : TCS , WIPRO , HCL TECH.

Analyzing firms in that industry / sector : As we have seen, Infosys has many competitors including TCS , WIPRO and HCL .

Here we can perform a financial analysis amongst other firms along with Infosys. In this way we can arrive at a verdict on whether we are investing in an appropriate company or not.

Name	CMP Rs.	P/E	Mar Cap Rs.Cr.	Div Yld %
TCS	3611.45	36.52	1335893.91	1.05
Infosys	1715.75	34.57	721560.57	1.57
Wipro	708.25	32.04	388179.02	0.14
HCL Technologies	1251.15	29.43	339520.21	1.76
Tech Mahindra	1430.80	28.86	138776.86	1.05

Above is an example how you can perform the peer comparison via seeing the financials of the competitors in the same sector.

It is very important to perform the peer comparison , As this shows the competitive structure of the industry and most importantly the efficiency of our investment proposition .

The analysis basically shows the financial performance of multiple firms at once who belong to a similar sector. Many parameters such as current price, market capitalization , ROCE , ROE , sales growth and other parameters can be seen and analyzed .

Further we would be performing the competitive analysis on the IT sector , looking at various market participants and their financials along with a " view based verdict "

SECTOR : IT & INDUSTRY : SOFTWARE

S.No.	Name	CMP Rs.	Debt Rs.Cr.	P/E	Mar Cap Rs.Cr.	Div Yld %	NP Qtr Rs.Cr.
1.	Mphasis	3356.70	513.45	49.07	62878.07	1.13	339.69
2.	L&T Technology	4851.65	0.00	66.94	51029.07	0.45	216.20
3.	Oracle Fin.Serv.	4729.45	69.76	22.57	40763.20	4.23	524.19
4.	Tata Elxsi	6318.30	73.21	95.36	39348.12	0.38	113.38
5.	Coforge	5604.85	1.40	68.05	33975.81	0.23	123.60

Even if we perform a basic comparison between these firms in the same sector , we will find that out of these 5 firms ,

- ORACLE FIN SERV = LOWEST P/E
- L&T TECH = ZERO DEBT FIRM
- TATA ELXSI = HIGHEST P/E
- COFORGE = LOWEST DIVIDEND
- MPHASIS = HIGHEST MARKET CAP

Even if you'd perform basic peer comparison you will find many pros-cons amongst the industry participants .

These pros-cons would help you to find the appropriate company based on qualitative , quantitative and valuation analysis .

We have seen that oracle finserv had the lowest P/E and the highest DIVIDEND YIELD amongst all the other players in the industry .

This shows that oracle was the undervalued firm amongst the other players in the industry as well as the dividend yield was highly attractive .

Financial intelligence

Financial intelligence refers to the knowledge a person must have in order to safeguard himself from getting manipulated by others.

In today's time period every person should have financial knowledge , and this does not mean to enroll in any advanced course , but basic and functional knowledge.

A person should have good knowledge about the following ,

- Investments
- Retirement & estate planning
- Insurance

Investments :

A person must invest some portion of his income in order to have a sustainable financial stability in future .

It is not necessary to invest everything you earn , but a portion of it gradually over a period of time .

Following are the investment avenues in which a person can invest ,

- Equity
- Debt securities
- Mutual funds
- ULIP
- PPF
- Pension funds

Retirement & estate planning :

Many of us want to have a stable and secured future ,
hence we plan for our retirement in our early income
earning days .

Retirement planning is a very essential financial planning
which a person must do and this includes a few simple
steps.

- Identifying goals
- Selecting appropriate retirement plan
- Gradually investing surplus income
- Utilizing proceeds in right way

Estate planning & succession refers to the distribution of
assets after a person passes away . This is generally
referred to as will.

It is very important for a person to make a will with a qualified legal consultant in order to make sure the assets which a person owns , are utilized by his successor effectively .

Example : Amit singh has 3 children ,wife and assets worth 10 CR . In case of death the assets are distributed as per the concerns of Amit without any legal disputes amongst others .

In case Amit passes away without making a will , then every relative , business partner will try to take over the assets through legal fights and no person will ever want this to happen .

Hence making a will is very essential for any person , rich or poor .

Insurance :

It is the most widely adapted method in order to be secured in case of an undesired event .

Most common insurance is health insurance , which is available for individual or family floaters.

When the person is in a state of earning stable income , he should purchase health insurance for himself and his family in order to safeguard the family in case of any event.

Fire insurance, marine insurance, home insurance are other few common types of insurance .

Case studies of past events

1) Enron (2001)

Prior to this debacle, Enron, a Houston-based energy trading company was, based on revenue, the seventh-largest company in the United States.

Through some complicated accounting practices that involved the use of shell companies, Enron was able to keep hundreds of millions worth of debt off its books.

Doing so fooled investors and analysts into thinking this company was more fundamentally stable than it actually was.

Additionally, the shell companies, run by Enron executives, recorded fictitious revenues, essentially recording one dollar of revenue, multiple times.

Eventually, the complex web of deceit unraveled, and the share price dove from over $90 to less than 30 cents. As Enron fell, it took down with it Arthur Andersen, the fifth leading accounting firm in the world at the time.

Andersen, Enron's auditor, basically imploded after David Duncan, Enron's chief auditor, ordered the shredding of thousands of documents.

2) WorldCom (2002)

Not long after the collapse of Enron, the equities market was rocked by another billion-dollar accounting scandal.

Telecommunications giant WorldCom came under intense scrutiny after yet another instance of some serious "book cooking."

WorldCom recorded operating expenses as investments. Apparently, the company felt that office pens, pencils, and paper were an investment in the future of the company and, therefore, expensed (or capitalized) the cost of these items over a number of years.

In total, $3.8 billion worth of normal operating expenses, which should all be recorded as expenses for the fiscal year in which they were incurred, were treated as investments and were recorded over a number of years.

This little accounting trick grossly exaggerated profits for the year the expenses were incurred.

In 2001, WorldCom reported profits of more than $1.3 billion. In fact, its business was becoming increasingly unprofitable. Who suffered the most in this deal? The employees; tens of thousands of them lost their jobs.

The next ones to feel the betrayal were the investors who had to watch the gut-wrenching downfall of WorldCom's stock price, as it plummeted from more than $60 to less than $1.

3) Tyco International (2002)

With WorldCom having already shaken investor confidence, the executives at Tyco ensured that 2002 would be an unforgettable year for stocks.

Before the scandal, Tyco was considered a safe blue chip investment, manufacturing electronic components, health care, and safety equipment.

During his reign as CEO, Dennis Kozlowski, who was reported as one of the top 25 corporate managers by *BusinessWeek*, siphoned hordes of money from Tyco, in the form of unapproved loans and fraudulent stock sales.

Along with CFO Mark Swartz and CLO Mark Belnick, Kozlowski received $170 million in low-to-no interest loans without shareholder approval.

Kozlowski and Belnick arranged to sell 7.5 million shares of unauthorized Tyco stock for a reported $430 million.

These funds were smuggled out of the company usually disguised as executive bonuses or benefits.

Kozlowski used the funds to further his lavish lifestyle, which included handfuls of houses, an infamous $6,000 shower curtain, and a $2 million birthday party for his wife.

In early 2002, the scandal slowly began to unravel and Tyco's share price plummeted nearly 80% in a six-week period. The executives escaped their first hearing due to a mistrial but were eventually convicted and sentenced to 25 years in jail.

4) HealthSouth (2003)

Accounting for large corporations can be a difficult task, particularly when executives want to falsify earnings reports.

In the late 1990s, CEO and founder Richard Scrushy began instructing employees to inflate revenues and overstate HealthSouth's net income.

At the time, the company was one of America's largest health care service providers, experiencing rapid growth and acquiring a number of other healthcare-related firms.

The first sign of trouble surfaced in late 2002 when Scrushy reportedly sold HealthSouth shares worth $75 million prior to releasing an earnings loss.

An independent law firm concluded the sale was not directly related to the loss, and investors should have heeded the warning.

The scandal unfolded in March 2003, when the SEC announced that HealthSouth exaggerated revenues by $2.7 billion.

The information came to light when CFO William Owens, working with the FBI, taped Scrushy discussing the fraud. The repercussions were swift as the stock fell 97% to a close of 11 cents in a single day.

CEO was acquitted of 36 counts of fraud but was later convicted on charges of bribery. Apparently, Scrushy arranged political contributions of $500,000, allowing him to ensure a seat on the hospital regulatory board.

5) Madoff investment scandal :

was a major case of stock and securities fraud discovered in late 2008. In December of that year, Bernie Madoff, the former NASDAQ chairman and founder of the Wall Street firm Bernard L.

Madoff Investment Securities LLC, admitted that the wealth management arm of his business was an elaborate multi-billion-dollar Ponzi scheme.

Madoff founded Bernard L. Madoff Investment Securities LLC in 1960, and was its chairman until his arrest.

The firm employed Madoff's brother Peter as senior managing director and chief compliance officer, Peter's daughter Shana Madoff as rules and compliance officer and attorney, and Madoff's sons Mark and Andrew.

Peter was sentenced to 10 years in prison, and Mark died by suicide exactly two years after his father's arrest.

Alerted by his sons, federal authorities arrested Madoff on December 11, 2008. On March 12, 2009, Madoff pleaded guilty to 11 federal crimes and admitted to operating the largest private Ponzi scheme in history.

On June 29, 2009, he was sentenced to 150 years in prison with restitution of $170 billion. He died in prison in 2021.

According to the original federal charges, Madoff said that his firm had "liabilities of approximately US$50 billion."[

Prosecutors estimated the size of the fraud to be $64.8 billion, based on the amounts in the accounts of Madoff's 4,800 clients as of November 30, 2008.

Ignoring opportunity costs and taxes paid on fictitious profits, about half of Madoff's direct investors lost no money.

Harry Markopolos, a whistleblower whose repeated warnings about Madoff were ignored, estimated that at least $35 billion of the money Madoff claimed to have stolen never really existed, but was simply fictional profits he reported to his clients

Investigators determined that others were involved in the scheme.

The U.S. Securities and Exchange Commission (SEC) was criticized for not investigating Madoff more thoroughly; questions about his firm had been raised as early as 1999.

The legitimate trading arm of Madoff's business that was run by his two sons was one of the top market makers on Wall Street.

Madoff's personal and business asset freeze created a chain reaction throughout the world's business and philanthropic community, forcing many organizations to at least temporarily close, including the Robert I. Lappin Charitable Foundation, the Picower Foundation, and the JEHT Foundation

Madoff started his firm in 1960 as a penny stock trader with $5,000 ($45,799 in 2021), earned from working as a lifeguard and sprinkler installer, and $50,000 that he had borrowed from his in-laws ($457,987 in 2021).

His fledgling business, which he founded with his high school sweetheart Ruth Alpern, began to grow with the assistance of his father-in-law, accountant Saul Alpern, who referred to a circle of friends and their families.

Initially, the firm made markets via the National Quotation Bureau's Pink Sheets. To compete with firms that were members of the New York Stock Exchange trading on the stock exchange's floor, his firm began using innovative computer information technology to disseminate quotes.

After a trial run, the technology that the firm helped develop became the NASDAQ.At one point, Madoff Securities was the largest buying-and-selling "market maker" at the NASDAQ.

He was active in the National Association of Securities Dealers (NASD), a self-regulatory securities industry organization, serving as the chairman of the board of directors and on the board of governors.

In 1992, Randall Smith of *The Wall Street Journal* described him as:

one of the masters of the off-exchange "third market" and the bane of the New York Stock Exchange. He has built a highly profitable securities firm, Bernard L.

Madoff Investment Securities, which siphons a huge volume of stock trades away from the Big Board.

The $740 million [$1.43 billion in 2021] average daily volume of trades executed electronically by the Madoff firm off the exchange equals 9% of the New York exchange's.

Mr. Madoff's firm can execute trades so quickly and cheaply that it actually pays other brokerage firms a penny a share to execute their customers' orders, profiting from the spread between bid and ask prices that most stocks trade for.

Several family members worked for him. His younger brother, Peter, was senior managing director and chief compliance officer, and Peter's daughter, Shana Madoff, was the compliance attorney.

Madoff's sons, Mark and Andrew, worked in the trading section , along with Charles Weiner, Madoff's nephew.

Andrew Madoff invested his own money in his father's fund, but Mark stopped in about 2001.

Federal investigators believe the fraud in the investment management division and advisory division may have begun in the 1970s.

However, Madoff himself stated his fraudulent activities began in the 1990s. Madoff's fraudulent activities are believed to have accelerated after the 2001 change from fractional share trades to decimals in the NYSE, which cut significantly into his legitimate profits as a market-maker.

With fractional trades Madoff profited up to 12.5 cents with each trade handled by his firm, but following decimalization this bid ask spread between sellers and buyers was reduced to as low as one cent.

In the 1980s, Madoff's market-maker division traded up to 5% of the total volume made on the New York Stock Exchange.

Madoff was "the first prominent practitioner" of payment for order flow, paying brokers to execute their clients' orders through his brokerage, a practice some have called a "legal kickback". This practice gave Madoff the distinction of being the largest dealer in NYSE-listed stocks in the U.S., trading about 15% of transaction volume.

Academics have questioned the ethics of these payments.

Madoff has argued that these payments did not alter the price that the customer received.

He viewed payments for order flow as a normal business practice: "If your girlfriend goes to buy stockings at a supermarket, the racks that display those stockings are usually paid for by the company that manufactured the stockings.

Order flow is an issue that attracted a lot of attention but is grossly overrated."

By 2000, Madoff Securities, one of the top traders of US securities, held approximately $300 million in assets ($472 million in 2021).

The business occupied three floors of the Lipstick Building in Manhattan, with the investment management division on the 17th floor, referred to as the "hedge fund", employing a staff of less than 24.

Madoff also ran a branch office in London that employed 28 people, separate from Madoff Securities.

The company handled investments for his family of approximately £80 million.

Two remote cameras installed in the London office permitted Madoff to monitor events from New York.

After 41 years as a sole proprietorship, Madoff converted his firm into a limited liability company in 2001, with himself as the sole shareholder.

6) Amaranth hedge fund :

One of the mistakes that led to Amaranth Advisors' multibillion-dollar losses on natural-gas investments is a common one in fast-shifting energy markets: confusing paper trading gains with cash profits.

The hedge fund's chief energy trader, 32-year-old Brian Hunter, misgauge when to take his chips off the table, losing roughly $5 billion in a week for a hedge fund that boasted world-class risk-management systems.

While Amaranth had traded energy for several years, its roots were in convertible-bond trading, a different, less-volatile market.

According to natural-gas investors who traded alongside Amaranth, Mr. Hunter repeatedly used borrowed money to double-down on his bets.

Buying more futures contracts of the kind his fund already owned supported their price by increasing demand, propping up paper gains, these traders say.

But that support only lasted as long as Amaranth and its lenders were willing to spend cash to buy more contracts. Such trades may also have masked growing weaknesses in market fundamentals, his trading peers say.

As Connecticut Attorney General Richard Blumenthal vowed to investigate the losses, the once-mighty Greenwich-based hedge fund is scrambling to explain to investors how its risk controls went awry, cutting its assets to about $4.5 billion, from $9 billion.

Working from Calgary, Alberta, Mr. Hunter employed a routine commodities strategy, exploiting the difference between the prices of contracts for delivery of natural gas at various future points.

He also was buying options to buy or sell natural gas at prices that others in the market thought unlikely but that would provide big payoffs if the prices came to pass.

Both strategies are supposed to be less risky than simply betting that prices will move either up or down.

In an Aug. 29 interview, when Mr. Hunter still had big paper gains, Amaranth founder and Chief Executive Nick Maounis said his bets were meant to minimize risk and maximize reward.

"Spreads and options are of their very nature instruments for positions which are designed to allow the user to capture upside with a much clearer understanding with respect to downside exposure," he said.

Mr. Maounis was unavailable yesterday. In a letter to investors Monday, he said the fund so far had met all demands for more cash to back trades and was unwinding natural-gas bets "to preserve investor capital."

An Amaranth spokesman declined to comment. Mr. Hunter has not responded to recent interview requests.

By early September, as prices fell precipitously because of a storage glut, Mr. Hunter held bets that would pay off exponentially only if natural-gas prices rebounded, either on the prospect of a cold winter or a nasty hurricane that hit natural-gas facilities.

But as evidence pointed to a meek hurricane season and mild winter, prices fell more.

Amaranth's systems didn't appear to measure correctly how much risk it faced and what steps would limit losses effectively.

The risk models employed by hedge funds use historic data, but the natural-gas markets have been more volatile this year than any year since 2001, making models less useful.

They also might not predict how much selling of one's stakes to get out of a position can cause prices to fall.

"It was a total failure of risk control to put your entire business at risk and not seem to know it," says Marc Freed, a managing director at Lyster Watson & Co.

an investment advisory firm that invests in hedge funds on behalf of clients but not with Amaranth.

"They were more leveraged than they realized."

Commodities trades require less margin money -- collateral to be surrendered in case of losses -- upfront than other markets.

On the main exchanges, traders typically post 10% of their position's value, whereas in the stock market, 50% is common.

So say, for example, gas is trading at $7 per million British thermal units and a trader buys one contract to buy or sell 10,000 million-BTUs for $70,000.

That trader posts just $7,000 to make that bet. If the price of gas goes down 10%, the trader has to post another 10%, or $7,000.

The trader now has $14,000 tied up in the market, and the value of his position has dropped to $63,000.

Compound that with generous lines of credit from banks, and it is easy for commodity hedge funds to get highly leveraged quickly.

Funds like Amaranth are able to borrow three to eight times their initial capital to make bets thousands of times over.

Mr. Hunter sometimes held 100,000 positions in a single contract, say traders familiar with his bets.

The volatile trading that distinguished Mr. Hunter was a departure for Amaranth. Denis Joseph, Amaranth's senior vice president for human resources until 2004, said Mr.

Maounis, the CEO, sought to centralize oversight of traders and to keep big discretionary trading authority on the fund's Greenwich trading floor. After big gains in 2005, Mr. Hunter was allowed to trade from Calgary.

"To have a relative newcomer …receive so much discretion is just shocking to me," Mr. Joseph said.

Still, the fund's high returns from energy last year and earlier this year were popular with its investors.

When Amaranth reported returns of roughly 12% in April, it told investors most of that profit was from energy trades.

 After Amaranth lost about 10% in May, or roughly $1 billion, mainly on energy trades, it told some investors that it was cutting back on leverage in the energy market, the investors say.

Mr. Hunter's bets ultimately went bad because he misjudged the movement of the difference between prices for different month contracts, known as the spread.

People familiar with the trades say he bet prices for nearby-month contracts months would fall and winter contracts would rise.

These people say he also presumed gas might be scarce in March if use was heavy this winter and prices would then fall off in April.

Amaranth. "We're extremely disappointed," said Brian White, its chief executive.

Fortunately for its investors, Paloma Partners, a $2.2 billion Connecticut firm, withdrew its money from Amaranth in late 2004, saying firm had grown too large.

Now other institutional investors are trying to do likewise.

Hedgebay Trading Corp A secondary market for trading hedge fund stakes, was inundated with calls from burned investors wanting to sell Amaranth stakes and bottom fishers looking to buy.

"Sellers want 30 to 40 cents on the dollar, but buyers are only willing to pay 10 cents to 20 cents on the dollar," said Hedgebay founder Jared Herman.

Conclusion :

One should be aware about the asset in which he is investing and should not invest blindly on someone's recommendation .

In today's time period there are thousands of schemes and lakhs of investment advisors , so one should know the basics of the financial markets before investing any amount .

Various investment avenues and their information have been given in previous chapters that will make you aware about the schemes , process & analysis so that no one can manipulate you .

Whether you belong to the finance field or not , you must ask a few basic questions to your advisor so that you will be safeguarded against any fraud .

Thank you

www.ingramcontent.com/pod-product-compliance
Lightning Source LLC
Chambersburg PA
CBHW082151230526

45467CB00044B/2913